Political Poetry

by

Lionel J. Seneviratne

Publisher - Lionel J. Seneviratne
4 Terrence Avenue
Mount Lavinia
Sri Lanka

FOREWORD

Poetry is one of the oldest forms of literature, and is still one of the most effective means of expressing not only a point of view but the poet's emotion and sensibility with regard his subject.

The author, Lionel Seneviratne, is a chartered civil engineer by profession who has lived in both Sri Lanka and the U.K. He is a keen observer of issues that affect us all such as global warming, political upheaval, and socialism.

The poems themselves fall into two categories. The first half of the poems were written in the latter half of 2010 and early 2011. They deal with diverse topics which range from the rise of democratic socialism to religion.

The later poems were mostly written in the early 1990s (unless otherwise noted) and were first published in his book also titled *'Political Poetry'*. Twenty years later the poems still serve as commentary on political issues both in Sri Lanka and the world in general.

While the poems are distinctly modern and sparse in their content - they raise universal issues that touch our daily lives and serve as food for thought.

Y. Seneviratne

June 2011

CONTENTS

Obama Has Arrived

Obama has arrived
At last he has realized
That China and India have arrived
They are no longer developing countries
They are economically independent countries
They give much aid to Sri Lanka
They do not need aid to develop
They are the future world
Europe and America are slowly going down
Capitalism is fast declining in the world
Democratic Socialism is the future.

(Written December 2010)

Democratic Socialism

Capitalism is fast declining
Communism is almost dead
Socialism is not a dirty word
Democratic Socialism as arrived
In fifty years a Democratic Socialist World
The private sector and the public sector will compete
In Sri Lanka already both sectors compete
Democratic Socialism is here to stay.

(Written December 2010)

A Democratic Socialist Country

In a Democratic Socialist Country
The private sector and the public sector compete
The rich people can go to the private sector
The poor and middle go to the public sector
Sometimes the rich also go to the public sector
Doctors in Govt. hospitals are more dedicated
Teachers in Govt. schools are more dedicated
In a Democratic Socialist World
Rich countries and poor countries will be friends.

(Written December 2010)

Destroy Our Forests Destroy the World

Forests are vital for every living creature
Forests absorb carbon dioxide and give out oxygen
Our industries give out only carbon dioxide
We breathe air and give out carbon dioxide
Over the last one hundred years
Oxygen content of air has fallen by thirty percent
The world will not end with a bang
But only a whimper.

(Written December 20th 2010)

Fonseka

There was a man called Fonseka
He became Army Commander
Of Sri Lanka's elite army
The army fought and defeated
The world's most evil terrorists LTTE
Fonseka worked from Colombo
Fonseka retired at sixty but was ambitious
He contested the presidency and lost
He tried to topple the democracy of
Mahinda Rajapakse and failed badly
He has been sentenced to three years
Rigorous imprisonment which he deserves

(Written September 2010)

A Personal God

Belief in a personal God created
An infinite and expanding universe
Seems impossible to fathom.
Whereas the force of karma in Buddhism
And the force of gravity according to Physics
Are far more logical to comprehend.
In our divided and rapidly deteriorating world
Buddhist philosophy rings true
A karmic force that rewards good
And brings destruction to evil
Is far more likely to govern
Like a world of unbridled consumption
With no regard for the environment
Bringing destruction upon itself.

(Written January 2011)

Ban Ki-moon

Ban Ki-moon is a capitalist stooge
He is only the Secretary General
His committee can only advise him
Sri Lanka was fighting the LTTE
The most ruthless terrorist organization
The Sri Lanka army protected civilians
They treated injured terrorists
After thirty years Sri Lanka is at peace
Sinhalese, Tamils, Muslims support the government
Ban Ki-moon might wreak the United Nations
Socialist countries might get together
And form the United Socialist Nations organization
The universal force of Karma prevails

(Written April 2011)

Sri Lanka
(Written in 1983)

If you should come across the seas to Sri Lanka
You will see an island paradise in Sri Lanka
A Democratic Government in Sri Lanka
A friendly and hospitable people in Sri Lanka

But now there is a terrorist problem in Sri Lanka
The Tamil terrorists want a separate state in Sri Lanka
The majority of Tamils are not separatists in Sri Lanka
Sinhalese, Tamils, and Muslims have lived peacefully in Sri Lanka
The President's grandchildren are half Tamil in Sri Lanka

The Sinhalese and Tamils are interdependent in Sri Lanka
A separate state is not viable in Sri Lanka
India does not support separatism in Sri Lanka
India wants unity in Sri Lanka.

Tamil youths want jobs in Sri Lanka
But they do not know Sinhalese or English in Sri Lanka
Narrow language policies of Government in Sri Lanka
Gave birth to terrorism in Sri Lanka.

Sri Lanka is a small island

Sri Lankans should learn the languages, English,
Sinhala, and Tamil

Only then will terrorism subside

In a decade in Sri Lanka.

(Previously published in 1990)

My Wish for the World

This world has lost its glory
Let's start a brand new story
Let's destroy nuclear weapons
Let's root out terrorism.

Let's ignore the color of a man's skin
After all what color is God's skin?
Black, White, Yellow, Brown all men are equal
Europeans, Asians, Africans all, all are equal.

Let rich nations help the poor nations
Let rich people help the poor people
Let's stop making weapons
Let's help the starving people.

Let's make Americans and Russians friends
Let them stop preparing for war
Let them divert their resources
To space travel with nuclear power.

This is our world
We are one world
Let us develop together

Or we'll just perish together.

(Previously published in 1990)

The Future and English

Why should neumonia be spelled pneumonia?
Why should dō be spelled dough?
Why should color be spelled colour?
The list is unending though
If English can be modified
To make it more phonetic
The next generation of computers
Will respond to oral words emphatic
Then humans will direct computers
Computers will direct robots
Robots will do the heavy work
Humans the light work do
Humans will not be
Materialistic – have much more time
To devote to prayer and meditation
Matters spiritual and sublime.
The world will be unified
All humans will be international
A Universal religion will evolve
With English, the language international.

(Previously published in 1990)

How Many Years

How many years must some communists exist

Before they realize the masses want Democratic
Socialism

How many years must some capitalists exist

Before they realize the masses want Democratic
Socialism.

How many years must some reactionary politicians exist

Before starving people precede weapons of mass
destruction

How many years must hundreds of thousands of
Scientists toil

Producing larger and larger weapons of mass
destruction.

How many years must a few Scientists toil

Before they learn how to create anti-matter

How many years must a few Scientists toil

Before they discover the unified field theory.

How many years must a few Scientists toil

Before they learn to harness the H-bomb reaction

The answer my friend depends on a few politicians

Will they unite or will they destroy the world?

(Previously published in 1990)

Help the Poor

It takes two to live in this world,
And they must have a child to see this world.
If they don't have their own child in this world,
They should adopt a poor child from a part of the world.

There are too many poor children in this world,
Adopt one child from this wide world.
And see the world through children's eyes,
You will see the beauty of in this world.

There are many poor people in this wide world,
There are also rich people in this divided world.
There are many rich countries in this wide world,
But there are more poor countries in this world.

The wealth of the world belongs to all,
The rich must help the poor in all.
Buddhism and Christianity preach this law,
Help the poor and avoid nuclear war.

(Previously published in 1990)

We Can See the Future

When I was just a little boy
My father passed away
World War two had broken out
I asked my mother what will be?

Will the Nazis rule the world?
Will nuclear bombs destroy the world?
Will all civilization be destroyed?
She replied what will be will be.

If you should die my little one
You will be reborn in a better world
The good die young, as they say
Do not be afraid my little one.

The future is ours to see
If we regularly meditate
We can develop technology
To solve all our problems.

We can create anti-matter
With the anti-matter force field
We can contain the H-bomb reaction

Solving our energy problems forever.

We can travel in space
On a mass scale using the anti-matter force field
We can colonize other planets
Venus can be a second earth.

(Previously published in 1990)

Young Engineers

Hello young engineers wherever you are
You have an ancient tradition rare
Your forefathers have built large dams
Your forefathers have built large temples.

Now in this technologically advanced age
You must work hard to keep up with the rest
You must learn English with the best
You must read widely like your seniors.

Gain your experience both here and abroad
Not depend on computers only
Use your intuition to solve problems
Appreciate technicians, give them a place.

Engineering is not only,
High math and computer programs.
Engineering is management,
Of men and materials.

Brave young engineers wherever you are
Not alone with your problems you are
Follow your seniors, you can't go wrong

We too were once, inexperienced engineers, young.

(Previously published in 1990)

Nuclear War

Regan's plan for Star Wars
A global arms race
Culminating in war in space
A desolated Earth in space.

A decimated human race
A disgusted 'God' above
A Karmic law operates
Weapons destroy civilizations.

I see a building or two
A school without children
A forest without animals
Oceans without life.

Who wins the nuclear war?
Not America! Not Russia!
No one wins the war
Everyone loses a nuclear war.

(Previously published in 1990)

Ron and Mikhail are Good Friends

Ron and Mikhail are very good friends
Nancy and Raisa are very good friends
Americans and Russians must be good friends
No cold war between good friends.

Americans and Russians fought together
To defeat a fascist Germany
They must now join together
To colonize Venus and Mars.

They are the hope of starving millions
Human rights of a few thousands
Must not hinder co-operation of friends
They must stop producing weapons
And help the starving millions.

(Previously published in 1990)

If Only

If only Reagan was more socialist
Gorbachev more democratic
The world would be more peaceful.

If Thatcher was more socialist
British miners wouldn't starve
British undergrads would get grants
Britain would be more united.

If Khomeini was less fanatical
And a little more permissive
Iran and Iraq would not fight
The Middle East would be peaceful.

If only J.R. was more socialist
And Sirimavo more capitalist
If U.N.P. and S.L.F.P. unite
And Prabhakaran be more democratic
Sri Lanka would be more peaceful.

(Previously published in 1990)

Why Must India Export Arms?

Rajiv plans large scale export of arms
These arms will be exported to poor countries
A high percentage will fall into terrorists' hands
So much for Non-Alignment and pancha seela.

Some arms will reach terrorists in Punjab and Jaffna
These arms will be used against Indian soldiers
Rajiv Ghandi's military policies
Are a disgrace to his mother and grandfather.

Indians and Hindus both believe in karma
Perhaps Rajiv does not believe in karma
The force of karma will operate
In the future Rajiv may fall from power.

(Previously published in 1990)

The 'U.N.' is a Weapon of Peace

The 'U.N.' faces bankruptcy soon
The 'U.S.' owes five hundred million
The 'U.S.' spends billions on weapons
The 'U.N.' is the best weapon of peace.

Reagan must promptly pay the dues
The 'U.N.' must precede Star Wars
If not history will label Reagan
As a president who betrayed the world.

(Previously published in 1990)

Benazir Must Liberate Muslim Women

She is the first to lead a Muslim nation
She must lead Muslim womankind
She must liberate Muslim women
She must bravely lead Pakistan.

She must be an example to women
She must stop wearing a veil
Muslim women must give up the veil
Benazir must lead the way.

Benazir and Rajiv must sign an accord
Let Pakistan and India be friends
Let there be peace in South Asia
Benazir must be a dove of peace.

(Previously published in 1990)

The Anti-Defamation Bill

Gandhi's Anti-Defamation Bill
Is a very unwise bill
It is an anti-democratic bill
He will be disgraced by such a bill.

Newspapers may defame individuals
But the Courts of Law are there
They must sue such newspapers
The courts will ultimately decide.

If such a bill is passed
Even wild rumors will be believed
Where there is smoke there is fire
The world will assume the worst.

(Previously published in 1990)

The World's Ecology is at Stake

The world's ecology is in danger
Atmospheric carbon dioxide is increasing
The 'green house' effect spells our doom
Erratic weather threatens every nation.

The United Nations must act now
Bush and Gorbachev must lead the world
Arms expenditure must be decimated
Funds must be diverted to grow trees.

Two billion acres of new forests are needed
Every family must plant a tree
The problem is acute but it is not too late
The world must awake and act now.

(Previously published in 1990)

About the Author

Lionel J. Seneviratne is a chartered civil engineer by profession qualified in the U.K. He has worked in both England and Sri Lanka as an engineer prior to retiring. He is the author of *'Political Poetry'* published in 1990 by Lake House Colombo and *'Karma, Rebirth, God and Computers We Are the Universe'* published in 1987 by the Vantage Press New York. He has written many articles, poems, and letters to newspapers in Sri Lanka and abroad over the years. An eloquent commentator on current affairs and politics, he resides in Mount Lavinia, Sri Lanka.

Other Works by the Author

Seneviratne, Lionel J. *Karma, Rebirth, God and Computers – We Are the Universe.* New York: Vantage Press, 1987. ISBN 0-533- 07145-3.

Seneviratne, Lionel J. *Karma, Rebirth, God and Computers – We Are the Universe.* Colombo: Sarvodaya Vishvalekha, 1987. ISBN 0-533-07145-3.

Seneviratne, Lionel J. *Political Poetry.* Colombo: Lake House Investments Ltd., 1990. ISBN 955-95295-0-1.

www.ingramcontent.com/pod-product-compliance
Lightning Source LLC
Chambersburg PA
CBHW060104050426

42448CB00011B/2622